SAVED FOR THE SERVICE OF GOD

Saved For
The Service
Of God

Biography of
Allister and Jean Shedden

by
Marion Cunningham

JOHN RITCHIE LTD
CHRISTIAN PUBLICATIONS

40 Beansburn, Kilmarnock, Scotland

ISBN-13: 978 1 909803 83 1

Copyright © 2014 by John Ritchie Ltd.
40 Beansburn, Kilmarnock, Scotland

www.ritchiechristianmedia.co.uk

Typeset by John Ritchie Ltd., Kilmarnock
Printed by Bell & Bain Ltd., Glasgow

Contents

Foreword

I count it an honour and a privilege to write these lines of introduction to this warm and detailed record of the lives and service rendered to the work of the Lord by Allister and Jean Shedden. All of their many friends, wherever found, will have fond memories stirred as these pages are read.

Allister made regular visits to Aberdeen when on furlough, with Jean accompanying him when family responsibilities allowed. It would have been in the sixties when I first met Allister and on a later furlough met Jean when my wife and I were able to have them both with us in our home. Each visit Allister made, each conversation held always ended with "Maranatha", evidence of the singleness of purpose and motivation in the varied aspects of service shared wholeheartedly by Jean. This focus has certainly been both a challenge and an encouragement to me and I am sure, to all who knew them. Since the main sphere of their service for the Lord over the whole of their married lives has been Honduras, this record rightly concentrates on that, however perhaps one personal experience will inform the reader that wherever Allister was found he always showed a deep sensitivity to the welfare of others.

Allister was invited to the Aberdeen New Year Conference on one occasion, which was held in a church building on the main thoroughfare. His host at that time had dropped Allister at the foot of the steps leading to the entrance. As he turned to mount the steps I was aware of him suddenly halting and turning his head. Two men drew level and Allister had detected they were speaking in Spanish. Thoughts of his responsibilities at the conference now would have to wait while he took advantage of this opportunity to converse with two obvious strangers to our city. The ensuing conversation revealed they were from a Spanish vessel in the harbour but since no unloading would be done over the holiday period they were simply filling in time. The conversation further revealed that they were believers from an assembly in the city of Vigo in Spain. The great joy experienced hugely encouraged these two brothers in Christ as they attended the gatherings, sharing fellowship with other believers, Allister had no difficulty translating for them!

On a lighter note we were informed at breakfast on one occasion that the bananas we produced for them were pretty tasteless, not really bananas, bananas should be black and the meat mushy, after all where else would you really know about bananas but in Honduras. Their preference was not shared by my family!!!

Many will join with me in thanking Marion for providing us with this lovely but seriously challenging record of lives lived with only obedience to the call of God and with only His honour in view.

E. Taylor

Prologue

Slowly the little plane began its descent. All that we could see below were millions of trees with the odd glimpse of a meandering river making its way through the rainforest jungle. As we continued with the descent, in the distance we spotted a small area that looked as if it had been cleared of trees and quickly realised that we were about to land and this was the 'airport'! As the wheels touched down my heart beat faster with anticipation, for this was to be my first visit to La Mosquitia Rainforest. As we stepped out of the 6 seater plane, we noticed a small wooden hut at the edge of the field; this was the terminal building! From the landing field we went straight to the river for the next leg of our journey in a dugout canoe. This part of the journey took an hour's paddling before we arrived at the very rickety dock. Indeed so rickety was it that we could not use it and the canoe was dragged to the bank so we could get out. There was no electricity, no running water and no other means of transport apart from how we had arrived! It was hard to believe that this was 2004 and not 1904!

The pier in La Mosquitia

La Mosquitia is a World Heritage site that contains the largest virgin rainforest north of the Amazon. Here, as a Tearfund Team, we would visit some of the remotest villages in Honduras where most of the people are indigenous Indians living in very primitive conditions. But God is at work in this area and we were greatly encouraged when we saw what the Lord had done through our partners, MOPAWI. Most of the people in the villages we visited were either Christians or certainly being exposed to the gospel.

So what was it that gave me the desire to become involved with the work of Tearfund and come to such a place as this? For me it was a double joy. Firstly it was a homecoming, as Honduras is the land of my birth and secondly, I had heard much about La Mosquitia from Uncle John Ruddock and others, but had never been able to go. At the time when I lived in Honduras it was very difficult to get there, as it was very remote and considered too dangerous a place to go. As a missionary kid or MK, my upbringing was completely unconventional and now as I look back, I can see that I have had life experiences that very few western children could ever even dream of. These experiences have shaped my life, given me the passion that I have for reaching out to and helping the poor, given me a second language, taught me that the colour of one's skin is of no importance and best of all taught me about a God of love and grace who loves each and every one of us equally, no matter our skin tone, culture, upbringing or status in society.

And so the short story that follows is a simple biography of the lives of two ordinary people whom God brought together, in an amazing way, to do extraordinary things for Him. It is the story of God's calling of Allister and Jean Shedden to serve Him in the land of Honduras, Central America in 1950 and it shows how God works in the lives of ordinary people to further His kingdom.

In writing this little book my main objectives were to keep it simple and not too detailed, but to say enough to capture a sense of who they are and how they allowed God to use them. It is also to ensure that Allister and Jean's family, immediate, extended and future, as well as their loyal friends and Christian supporters, remember them for what God has done through them over the course of their lives. The time spent talking with Mum and Dad and my sisters, reminiscing about our lives in Honduras, the friends we made, the experiences we had, have been very precious to me and I know that my sisters have also found those moments precious too. We have shared with each other. We have spoken with some of Mum and Dad's friends of many years and with many of the lovely folks from Honduras who grew to love and respect them over their 40 plus years living in Honduras. The little tape recorder that Dad and I used to capture our reminiscing will remain a treasure for me as I can listen to his and Mum's voices as we talked, laughed and sometimes nearly cried together.

I have grown to love, respect and admire them more and more as I gathered the information. So often as children, we grow up knowing only the parents that we see during our childhood and then in their old age and often not taking the time to truly get to know them as individuals and as they were in their youth. I thank God on a daily basis for the unconditional love, guidance, teaching, training, support and example that they have consistently shown me, my sisters, our husbands, children, grandchildren and now even great grandchildren.

They have stood beside each one of us in our own circumstances, gently guiding us and praying with and for us and I will never be able to thank them enough for leading us to know the Lord whom they love and serve. It has been a privilege writing this little book and I hope that as you read it you too will be blessed.

Honduras will always have a place in my heart as it does for them and my two sisters and even for many of our children.

Over the ninety years of their lives, Allister and Jean have established many lifelong friendships that have not only spanned the years, but which have also spanned continents and cultures. They have befriended their missionary colleagues and fellow Christians in Honduras, Scotland and Canada, as well as countless strangers whom they met along the way. Only eternity will reveal the true extent of their impact on the lives of those with whom they have come into contact.

I know that I would be failing them if I did not make it clear that this is not about what 'they' have done, but about what God has done. I am sure that they would echo the words from Psalm 115 verse 1:

'Not to us O LORD, not to us, but to Your name be the glory, because of Your love and faithfulness.'

First view of the rainforest

Local airstrip at La Mosquitia

CHAPTER ONE

The Story Begins

On the 5th January 1924, Jane Reid Baird Morton entered the world. She was the first daughter born to Agnes Baird and Frank Morton. The family lived in Argyll Road, Saltcoats when Jane was born, but shortly after Frank went to the United States and found work as a butler to a very wealthy American family. Later his wife Agnes and young daughter Jane moved to Hamilton, Ontario in Canada, where Frank had found work with a large company called Westinghouse. It was there in Canada that Jane's sister Emma and brother, Frank, were born. The family lived in Canada for the first nine years of Jane's life only returning to Scotland due to the global depression that had hit. The family did not go back to Canada and after they settled back in Scotland, two younger sisters, Agnes (Nan) and Martha, were added to the family.

Only a few months later, on the 8th April 1924, in Christie Gardens, Saltcoats, Allister Robert Shedden made his appearance. He was the third child, but first son, born to Marion Shearer and Robert Ritchie Shedden. Allister's two older sisters were Annie and May and later two more boys were added to the family, Ian and later Ritchie. Robert Shedden was a butcher and the family owned a butcher's shop in Glasgow Street in Ardrossan. Allister still remembers those days when as a youngster, he would go with his father to get pigs for butchering and watched his father skin and chop up the meat. He would also earn a few pennies by helping a local merchant with his deliveries from a horse and cart. It is amazing to think of the changes that both Jane and Allister have witnessed in their lifetime. From horses and carts to fancy cars; from crackly radios to 3D televisions; from single records to CDs; from computers that took up the space of a large room to computers that sit in the palm of your hand. These changes and many more have taken place during their life time. In 1903 the Wright brothers invented the first powered flying machine and in 1927, Charles Lindbergh first flew solo across the Atlantic. Yet by 1939, airplanes were a vital weapon in the war. With rapid technological advancement came the huge machines that we all take for granted today. When the war broke out Robert went to work in ICI in Stevenston as the butcher in the work's canteen. Many hundreds of people, mainly women, were playing their part in the war effort by making ammunition, so his role as butcher was a vital one.

Little did Jane and Allister know what God had planned for their lives! Born only streets apart, they were later to meet, marry and live a life together that was, to put it mildly, certainly not the normal route taken by newly-wed Scots couples.

However, before we get to that point, we need firstly to learn a little more about their early lives.

On her return from Canada, Jane (now known as Jean) went to Wilson Primary School in Saltcoats, where the Head Mistress asked a young girl to look after her while she settled into Scotland. That young girl was called Betty Murray and until Betty was called home in May 2013, they remained firm friends. This included Jean being bridesmaid at Betty's wedding. By now Frank, Jean's father had a nursery and when she grew up Jean went to work in her father's floral business and there learned to make wedding bouquets and wreaths for funerals, as well as general floral decorations. Jean always had an interest in medicine but was not able to pursue her dream to become a Doctor or Nurse. Jean and her family were committed Christians who attended their local Brethren

Assembly and Jean committed her life to the Lord at around 13 years of age.

Later while working at A.K. Young's grocery business, Jean noticed the very handsome young man who worked in his uncle's plumbing business just across the road from the shop. Allister too had noticed the lovely Jean and was very interested in her, though at that point they were merely acquaintances and admired each other from the distance.

When the war broke out in 1939, the ICI plant in Stevenston became one of the very important centres where the war effort was aided as it was there that ammunition was made for use by the troops. When they were old enough, Jean and her sister Emma, went to work in ICI, so that they too could contribute to the war effort.

Allister's family had moved from Saltcoats to neighbouring Ardrossan where Allister attended Winton Primary School and from there went on to Eglington Secondary School. On leaving school at 14, Allister became apprenticed to his Uncle James Shedden who had a plumbing and slating business. After 2 ½ years with his uncle, Allister went on to continue his 6 year apprenticeship at the shipyard in Ardrossan, but in 1939 World War II began and life changed for everyone.

CHAPTER TWO

The War Years

Although employees of the ship-building industry were exempt from the Armed Forces, there was great demand for flight-crews for the Royal Air Force, and one could volunteer either as pilot or navigator. Allister volunteered to train as a pilot in the R.A.F. After the preliminary medical exams, at the age of 18½, he was eventually called for service in February 1943 and sent to Earls Court, London, where he was given the necessary inoculations, as well as his uniform and other essential kit. After being in London for four weeks, he was then sent to Brighton on the south coast of England for basic drill training. Air raids by the German Luftwaffe were constant, and on many occasions, the planes would cross the English Channel just a few feet above the water to strafe and bomb the buildings of Brighton.

From Brighton, all the aircrew candidates were then sent to Newquay, in Cornwall, England where they would be schooled in the various subjects related to all aspects of aviation, such as D.R/Astro Navigation, Morse code, Meteorology, airframes and engines, all types of weaponry, etc. This intensive course lasted more than nine months with the respective exams on the varied subject matter. All successful candidates were then sent to grading school at Desford, England, where the candidates were given a maximum of 12 hours flying instruction. This was to test the aptitude of each one, as to whether the candidate was suitable to continue as a pilot, navigator or airgunner. After 8 hours training, Allister went solo, and accordingly, was chosen to continue for pilot training. Those who failed this rigorous screening, became navigators, gunners and bomb aimers.

After grading school, all successful candidates were then sent to a Holding Unit at Heaton Park, Manchester, England, awaiting posting to one of the Commonwealth countries for further training according to their grading. Allister found himself in a group that was chosen to go to South Africa, and after a lengthy stay at Heaton Park, they were on their way to Greenock in Scotland, to join the troopships taking them to South Africa. By now Allister was 19½ years of age and he was to find himself at sea on the troopship for 7 weeks.

At this point in Allister's story we take a short detour to fill in some details that were the turning point in Allister and Jean's lives. Allister had been brought up in a church going and God fearing family, attending church and Sunday School regularly. However, during this time he never heard the message that he needed to experience a personal relationship with God and so although he was never drawn to drinking and gambling as many of his peers were, neither did he give God much time or place in his life. Then God stepped in and changed Allister's life forever. The following is Allister's own personal testimony of how God intervened.

"I was very much a loner with few friends and kept to myself. Drinking, gambling, smoking and similar other attractions had no appeal to me. I was too much a lover of sports like running, football and swimming to indulge in these body destroying habits. On leaving school, I entered the work force as an apprentice plumber. However, in the year 1939 the war clouds gathered on the horizon, and then the Second World War commenced. At this point in time I was employed in a local shipyard at my trade as apprentice plumber. Such employment was considered to be a reserved occupation, exempting one from being called up for the Armed Forces. There was only one arm of the Forces that had higher priority, and that was if one volunteered to be either a pilot or navigator in the Royal Air Force. I volunteered as a pilot, and after all the preliminaries and medical exams, I soon found myself as a cadet pilot studying the various basic courses necessary for a flying career. This covered the first year of my training, at the end of which I was posted to South Africa to do my actual flying training. This meant a long arduous voyage on a troopship in seas that were then infested with U-boats. Prior to boarding the troopship on the river Clyde in Scotland, I was in the city of Manchester, and as I was walking along one of the streets, someone handed me a gospel booklet entitled "SAFETY, CERTAINTY AND ENJOYMENT" which was immediately stuffed into one of the deepest pockets of my uniform.

Our convoy of 26 ships formed in the mouth of the river Clyde, and at a convenient hour we set sail at the speed of the slowest ship in the convoy. As we moved into the Atlantic ocean, I became more and more afraid, for I knew that if anything were to happen and I died in these frigid waters, I was NOT READY TO MEET GOD! Then I remembered the gospel booklet in my pocket. This I read and reread, and was brought under the conviction of sin. Then one night I saw a young man reading his Bible, and speaking to him, asked if he would kindly explain to me what he was reading. At that, he invited me to accompany him to a Bible study that was being held on board the ship. I found about thirty five or forty young servicemen like myself in the study, and I knew right away that they had something that I did NOT have. Though the study was on the gospel by John, yet I was convicted, not by any particular verse of Scripture, but by the LIVES OF THOSE WHO WERE THERE in the study. I kept asking myself, "What do they have that I do not have?" Night after night I attended the study, then after zig-zagging for three weeks in the Atlantic without mishap, the convoy passed through the Straits of Gibraltar into the Mediterranean Sea. On the second day after passing Gibraltar, we were attacked by the German Air Force. That night 13 ships of our convoy were sunk. Our ship was not hit despite one pilot firing a torpedo at us - it missed! The loss of life that night was high including two men on our ship who were killed when one of the pilots strafed our ship with machine gun fire.

Had that torpedo hit its mark, I would have had no chance of survival, as I was on the very bottom hold of the ship. And I WAS NOT THEN SAVED! To this day I testify that it was the hand of God that diverted the torpedo from striking and sinking our ship, because TWO NIGHTS LATER I trusted in the Lord Jesus Christ as my Saviour and Lord. Standing on the deck of the ship on the night of the 11th November 1943, I committed my soul into the Saviour's hand, passing from death and fear, to salvation and peace with God. I promised the Lord that I would serve Him according to His will. Later on, the Lord revealed to me that He wanted me to serve Him on the mission field."

On his arrival in South Africa Allister and the other pilots in training, went to begin their Elementary training in Benoni in the Transvaal, South Africa. This training involved further intense study including 80 hours of flying in single motor planes called the Tiger Moth. Actually this was a grading school when successful pilots who completed the course were divided into either fighter or bomber categories to go on to advanced flying at two different flying schools. Allister was assigned as a bomber pilot and accordingly moved on to the Secondary Flying School at Dunnotter, still in the Transvaal. His flying would now be on a twin motor plane called the Airspeed Oxford and the course consisted of more studying, longer cross-country flights, night flying and practice bombings, etc. On graduating as a pilot Allister had now flown approximately 280 hours.

In the town of Springvale Allister and his good friend George Shenton, who had been with him right from the beginning of their call-up to serve in the R.A.F., were befriended and welcomed into the home of a family called Heneke, where they enjoyed warm hospitality when they were not on duty. They also enjoyed going to church services with them as most Sundays were duty free. However, George and Allister were later separated as George was graded to train as a fighter pilot while Allister was graded to continue as a bomber pilot. They did however, still manage to see a lot of each other during their respective courses. As the Heneke family lived fairly close to the Air-school where Allister was training, he continued to enjoy their warm hospitality. On the day of his graduation as a pilot gaining his wings, the Heneke family was present at the ceremony.

Allister Shedden

Having been awarded his wings, Allister still had further training to complete. The newly graduated pilots were taken onboard a Sunderland Flying Boat at Cape Town en route to Cairo in Egypt and then on to Palestine where the training was in the twin motor Wellington bomber. It was at this advanced flying school that Allister had to "crew up" with those who, once they were chosen, would remain as his crew till the end of the war. He had to pick a flight engineer, a navigator, a bombardier, a wireless operator and three gunners. At this school the training consisted of working together as a responsible crew and becoming familiar with the aircraft and escape routes, for most of their training would be night flying on longer cross-country flights of 4 to 5 hour duration. After completing 80 flying hours on the Wellington bomber, they were sent to the country of Egypt where they would be flying four motor Liberator bombers. From there they were moved to the war zone in Italy. All of this took a period of two to three years but as the war was nearing its end, Allister and his crew were not called upon to do any bombing during their time in Italy. When the war finally ended, Allister's crew was transferred back to Palestine. However, Palestine was in turmoil as the Jews who were returning to Palestine found that Britain, which had promised them a homeland there, failed to make good on its promise, so under the leadership of Zionist Menachen Begin they resorted to terrorism. One of the targets was to do as much damage as possible to the R.A.F. planes stationed in Palestine. All planes were ordered out of Palestine and regrouped in Egypt where all the Liberator bombers would eventually be returned to the U.S.A. under the lease/ lend agreement. Allister and his crew were assigned to a Squadron that flew Lancaster bombers, so once again they had to familiarize themselves with this new aircraft that was quite different from the Liberator. The R.A.F. began to scale back the different squadrons to peace-time strength which meant flying the aircraft back to the U.K. All told, Allister made three such trips from Cairo to Gloucester, England to leave the aircraft at stipulated Maintenance Units. Allister was officially demobilized from the R.A.F. in February 1947 having completed four years of war-time service.

When it came time for him to go home he had to make the lengthy journey by ship. However, he gave God thanks that the only bombing he had to do was practising during his training.

CHAPTER THREE

New Horizons

Having kept in touch with his lovely Jean via letters and having told her of his conversion, the romance really took off and on the 17th of September 1947, Allister and Jean were married! They began married life in Saltcoats and attended the Assembly in Ardrossan. From the beginning Jean knew that Allister had dedicated himself to God's work and that he felt called to the mission field. On the 16th October 1949 Agnes Baird Shedden was born, the first of three daughters born to Allister and Jean.

Emma (Jean's sister), Allister, Jean, Ian (Allister's brother)

In 1950 Allister and Jean, being commended by both Ardrossan and Saltcoats assemblies, set off with little Agnes, now one year old, on the long journey to the little known country of Honduras in Central America. It was there that Mr and Mrs John Ruddock were serving the Lord as missionaries and as Nettie Ruddock was Jean's aunt, it was largely due to hearing from them about the needs of that country, that Allister and Jean felt the Lord's calling to Honduras. The journey was made by ship and after saying their farewells to family and friends; they set sail for New York, a five day journey. On arrival in New York they were met by Allister's Aunt Margaret and her husband and during their stay in New York they visited the Assembly on 73rd Street and got to know many of the Christians there. They remained lifelong friends with the Robinson family from that assembly. They also met with Jean's Aunt Emma who was so horrified at the idea of them taking the beautiful little Agnes to such a backward country, that she begged them to leave Agnes with her so that she could bring her up with her and her husband, Uncle Ben. Needless to say that did not happen and the little family set off once again by ship to complete their journey to Honduras.

Aunt Emma, Uncle Ben, Jean and Inez

This proved to be a very uncomfortable five days, as they hit a hurricane causing the ship and its passengers to be tossed around mercilessly. Thankfully they arrived safely in Guatemala from where they sailed to a small town in Honduras called Puerto Cortes. And so began for real, the new life to which God had called them in the land of Honduras.

Jean and Inez on route to Honduras

CHAPTER FOUR

Honduras - The Land of Adoption

Honduras is a beautiful, diverse country with a wealth of natural beauty and resources. It was discovered by Christopher Columbus in 1502. On the eastern coast are idyllic, white sandy beaches, lapped by the clear blue Caribbean Sea and dotted with shady palm trees laden with the most delicious fresh coconuts. One would be hard pushed to find better beach locations anywhere in the world. Around the Bay Islands there can be few places that could boast of better diving amongst the coral reefs and swimming beside the colourful tropical fish.

Bay Islands, Honduras

To the South west there is a short coast line with the Pacific Ocean. Honduras has borders with Nicaragua to the South, Guatemala to the North and El Salvador to the west.

Much of the country was covered in dense jungle offering a rich habitat to myriads of unique and colourful wildlife, flora and fauna. Sadly, since the arrival of the United Fruit Company, which scythed through the jungles and cleared vast areas of forest to develop banana plantations for export around the world, the deforestation has caused havoc with the natural beauty and habitats of its wildlife. Railway lines were laid and as insecticides were used liberally to protect the bananas, the land became decimated.

Today Honduras and its people have suffered mud slides and flooding, devastation and death, when hit by the frequent hurricanes that come on an almost annual basis, because the trees that once would have protected them are long gone.

Honduras is rich in timber, gold, silver, copper, lead, zinc, iron ore, antimony, coal, fish and hydropower. Sadly many of these resources have been taken over by multinational companies who do not put much back into the economy of the country and exploit the workers, thus causing the level of poverty among so many with the increasing wealth of a few.

Today, Honduras is the second poorest country in Central America and one of the poorest countries in the Western Hemisphere, with an extraordinarily unequal distribution of income and massive unemployment. It is banking on expanded trade under the US-Central America Free Trade Agreement (CAFTA) and on debt relief under the Heavily Indebted Poor Countries (HIPC) initiative.

Despite improvements in tax collections, the government's fiscal deficit is growing due to increases in current expenditures and financial losses from the state energy and telephone companies. Honduras is the fastest growing remittance destination in the region with inflows representing over a quarter of GDP, equivalent to nearly three-quarters of exports. The economy relies heavily on a narrow range of exports, notably bananas and coffee, making it vulnerable to natural disasters and shifts in commodity prices. However, investments in non-traditional export sectors are slowly diversifying the economy. Growth remains dependent on the economy of the US, its largest trading partner, and on reduction of the high crime rate, as a means of attracting and maintaining investment.

There is presently one area protected by the government and registered as a World Heritage Site and that is the virgin rainforest of La Mosquitia. This is a wonderful jungle, inhabited by creatures large and small. Huge butterflies with the most amazing iridescent colours and brilliant patterns, iguana, leatherback turtles, insects, beetles and bugs and a myriad of other rare wildlife.

Yet, even with the protection offered, this magnificent jungle is being encroached by illegal loggers and ranchers who care little for the unique value of this small corner of our world.

Meandering River

It was into this country that Allister and Jean stepped intrepidly to begin the work that they felt God had called them to do. Here they would serve God and their fellow man by showing and telling God's great plan of salvation not only in words but more importantly by the way they lived.

They grew to love and be loved by the wonderful people that they came into daily contact with and with whom they were able to share the gospel.

Group of ladies

CHAPTER FIVE

The Early Days

Honduras in the early 1900s was a dark, difficult, Godless environment. Violence, corruption and terrible poverty prevailed. The climate was hot and humid with two main seasons; the wet season and the dry season. Life was hard! Into this harsh place came the light of God's word in the person of Alfred Hockings. Although Alfred was an Englishman, he took on a job with the American Bible Society to distribute bibles in the whole of Central America; there being no Americans who would take that job! He had a helper and together they travelled with two mules one to carry Alfred and the other to carry bibles. They would often be robbed, traverse dangerous routes and almost inevitably, he succumbed to malaria. After a number of years doing this work he felt called to become a full time missionary in Honduras. Returning to England, he married and came back to Honduras in 1911 with his new wife Evelyn. The pioneering work in Honduras had begun and in 1930 John and Nettie Ruddock came to Honduras having served the Lord for 4 years in Guatemala. In 1936 The National Bible Society of Scotland reported the following: "Honduras is one of the most needy of the Central American Republics. Politically, the country is always seething with unrest, while a lack of roads and railways to connect up a sparse population scattered over mountainous country of 46,000 square miles makes missionary work a difficult task. The workers are few, widely separated, and the whole environment is unsympathetic towards a religious life."

Alfred Hockings and his colleague Sergio Caller

And so it was into this environment that Allister and Jean began their new lives as missionaries in Honduras. Life in their early days in Honduras was not easy. Firstly they had to learn Spanish and this was to take a number of years before they were confident and competent. However, they found a school teacher who was willing to teach them the language if they in turn would teach her English. For roughly nine months they struggled with their lessons and then little by little, it all began making sense. They found they could read the language a lot quicker than they could speak it. The conjugation of the verbs was the most difficult part of the learning process but after three years or so even verbs yielded to their quest to speak the language without having to resort to a bi-lingual dictionary. To gain confidence in speaking the language Allister started by reading portions of the Scriptures and then little by little took more and more part with short messages until he was able to think fluently in Spanish. Altogether it took them five years to be able to master the Spanish language and speak with more fluency.

From his years in the RAF in Egypt, South Africa and Palestine, Allister had become somewhat used to encountering various tropical creatures and the oppressive heat, but poor Jean had to become used to the terrible heat, the cockroaches, scorpions, snakes, mosquitoes and many other insects and animals native to Honduras. For many years they had no running water and poor, if any electricity, so life was especially difficult with a young child. On one particular occasion Allister and Jean found that they had no money and little Agnes, who was now called Inez and who was three years of age, discovered that they had no food and even the milk was gone. There was only one thing left to do and that was to commit the problem to The Lord in prayer. Very soon after they had finished praying there came a knock at the door and when Jean went to the door there stood a young lady who explained that a couple Doña Moncha and Don Raphael had felt led to send the girl with a few groceries for Allister and Jean. This couple had recently joined them in the Assembly having moved from the coast and they had opened a tiny little shop. From the little that they had they gave willingly to the family without knowing their particular circumstances. God certainly moves and provides in unexpected ways. The following day when Allister went to the post office there was a letter with a cheque from fellow missionaries, John and Nettie Ruddock. How amazing is our God!

During their years in Honduras Allister suffered more than one incidence of malaria with Jean suffering from dengue fever. Both are caused by the mosquito, and both can be very dangerous. Thanks to God, they recovered and were able to continue their work; although for many years there were lingering problems caused by these diseases.

Although not very much better today, at that point in time, roads were unpaved and in very poor condition, especially after a down-pour of rain, so travel in the early days was hard. Deep ruts were formed by heavy trucks, and smaller vehicles would get stuck in the mud turning even a short journey into a nightmare. Journeys involved travel by various means, horseback, dugout canoe, train, on foot or sometimes by MAF planes and local airline planes.

A rutted road after rain

Shortly after arriving in the country, Allister and Jean were invited to join a senior missionary, James Scollon, on a visit to a Moreno (descendants of African slaves) village which meant travelling by dugout canoe, and crossing a lagoon which was a habitat of Cayman (a tropical American crocodile). This did not make for a very relaxed journey! To avoid travelling in the blazing sun for four hours, the practice was to set off at two o'clock in the morning. As the dawn began to break, Mr. Scollon shouted, "Here comes a crocodile," and sure enough they saw what appeared to be a crocodile in the early morning mist. However, the "crocodile" turned out to be a half-submerged tree, much to the relief of the intrepid couple as they stepped ashore on the other bank of the lagoon. This was the halfway mark on the journey to the village. Another four hours would be spent on the back of a mule through heavy under-brush with clouds of mosquitoes to keep them company. Horseback riding was almost always on mules as they were more sure-footed than horses. For Jean and the other lady missionaries this was done side saddle, so the element of comfort was non-existent, as the mules made their way up steep hillsides. Jim Scollon together with his wife Olive, had arrived in Honduras from Guatemala around 1938.

Following these very early pioneering days a number of other younger missionaries began to arrive in Honduras and God's word and work began to take roots. Prior to Allister and Jean's arrival, Alfreda Hockings, daughter of Alfred and Evelyn, was commended to full time work in 1948; Eva Johnston, another single sister from Northern Ireland, came in 1949; and they were followed by Allister and Jean in 1950. Later Jim and Vera Pugmire from England came in 1951; Bill and Kay Tidsbury from Canada in 1952; and Sam and Edna Hanlon from Scotland in 1955. These young missionary couples became firm friends and each used their gifts to full effect. As well as preaching and teaching, Sam Hanlon used his skills to help many widows and very poor families to build or repair their homes, and as noted later in the story, Sam returned with Allister to help rebuild homes and churches following the devastating hurricane of 1974. Edna Hanlon was also a great asset in the work as she used her nursing skills to help many women safely deliver healthy babies. The poor people could not afford medical help and so both the infant mortality and maternal mortality rates were very high. Edna no doubt helped to save many babies and mothers from unnecessary death. Until both Sam and Edna went home to be with the Lord, the two couples remained very good friends.

Bill Tidsbury and Allister travelled together evangelising in the remote mountainous areas of the interior. Most of the earlier assemblies had grown in the coastal towns of Tela, San Pedro and La Ceiba. Allister and Jean were the first to go into the interior, more mountainous region of the country. Bill was a great evangelist and he and his wife Kay worked mainly in the town of El Progreso. This was the area where the United Fruit Company had set up their banana plantations and Bill was often to be found evangelising the local plantation workers and also the American bosses. There were four helicopter pilots working for the Banana Company spraying the crops with pesticides. Bill would regularly speak with them and before long all four became Christians and long term friends. These four pilots helped Bill and the local Christians, both physically and financially, to build a Hall where they could hold the meetings in El Progreso. Many of the plantation workers became Christians and on occasions some of the plantation accommodation was used to hold camps for the young people. Kay and Jean became lifelong friends and even to this day they remain in communication and see each other when they can. Together they worked with the women; teaching them from God's word as well as teaching them practical skills.

Shortly after the arrival of Sam and Edna, Stan and Esma Hanna from USA came in 1958. While the number of missionaries in Honduras was growing, many were stationed in areas that were remote from their colleagues and so the work was often lonely. Honduras is a vast, mountainous country and the infrastructure was not good, so travel was dangerous.

A single lady, Ruth Atkins, from England came around 1963 and for a time lived with the Shedden family. She later married a Honduran Christian call Luis Maya and they eventually returned to England where they still live at the time of writing. Today there are three missionary couples who remain in Honduras. They are: David and Lourdes Domingez, who arrived from Argentina in 1975, followed by the Woolers in 1980 and the Haesemyers in 1989. The rest of the work is in the hands of national workers and local church leaders and is continuing to grow and show fruit.

At the time of Allister and Jean's arrival (1950) the President of the country was an ex-general of the army, General Tiburcio Carias. When he stepped down from the presidency, a hand-picked member of General Carias' political party took over. The opposing political party cried foul, claiming that they had won the elections. There was always bitter rivalry between the political parties, and the party in power had no intention of handing the presidency to the opposition. This caused much unrest among the politicians and a revolution ensued with many civilians being killed in different parts of the country. On one occasion Allister was caught in the crossfire when he was on his way home, but fortunately was not hit. Another time they had a soldier with a machine-gun outside their bedroom window firing down the street and again they were caught in the crossfire as the other side fired back. Only the goodness of the Lord protected them from harm. No fewer than 11 revolutions took place between 1955 and 1978. Since then there has been more stability and a more democratic approach.

A number of the missionaries and the Nasrallas

CHAPTER SIX

Settling into a New Way of Life

In the first year home was in the coastal town of Tela at the Ruddock's house, while they went to the USA on furlough. In 1951 the family move to Tegucigalpa, the capital which is in the interior of the country. Manuel Nasralla, a Christian Palestinian, and his wife, Anna, with their two little daughters, Judy and Ruth, had a small church of around 10 believers, meeting in their home. So, Allister, Jean and Inez joined this little group of Christians and thus began the lifelong friendship between Manuel, Allister, Anna and Jean. This friendship has not only continued across the years but also in the succeeding generations and across many miles.

Allister and Jean rented a derelict two story house in a very poor district and living in the upper part of the house, they were able to use the largest of the rooms downstairs for the meetings. It was into this house that Marion Shearer, second daughter and yours truly, was born on the 30th September 1952.

Some of the members of that first Assembly in Tegucigalpa

Once they had cleaned up and made the property habitable, the first task Allister had was to make benches for the little church and then he proceeded to visit the homes around the area inviting people in to hear the gospel message. The Church grew in numbers over the next few years until finally they were able to buy a plot of land in 1955 and build the first Church building in Tegucigalpa.

About this time a Christian family from La Ceiba, who had a very large family and little income, sent their daughter Nora to live with Allister and Jean. In return for her room and board, Nora would do a little house work and care for Inez and daily go to the local well to collect water. There was little running water at this point in the poor area where Allister and Jean were living, so it had to be collected regularly and it was quite a walk down the hill and back up to the house. Nora and Inez would walk down together. In the early 1950s there were not too many blond, white children around and so when they were together the people called them "café con leche" which is "coffee and cream"!

Cafe con leché

Due to the recession back home in the UK, finances were very tight and there were times when the family had neither money nor food. Allister had to put his flying skills to good use to support his growing family. He became a pilot for a local airline called SAHSA. Oftentimes he had to land on very short dangerous airstrips and even the main airport in Tegucigalpa is today noted as the second most dangerous airport in the world for pilots to land at. However, this job allowed him to support the family and also to be able to help financially with the church building. Manuel Nasralla was one of the main people who helped to fund the building of this little church.

However, prior to the building of the hall, Allister and Jean returned to Scotland on their first furlough five years after their initial departure to Honduras to report to their commending assembly of what had then been achieved.

Shortly after returning to Honduras in 1956, the work of building the hall was commenced. Many of the Christians from the little congregation were in the building trade and so with their help the hall was built. Allister would often work as a pilot during the morning and then come back home, swapping his pilot's uniform for old clothes and armed with whatever tools were required, set off to help with the building in the afternoons. The hall was finally completed and inaugurated in 1956 and this was the first Assembly building in Tegucigalpa.

Building in progress

Completed building

Interior of the new hall

Some members of the Assembly

In 1957 Allister and Jean managed to purchase a plot of land on which they were able to build a small but lovely family home in an area of Tegucigalpa called Alameda. Manuel Nasralla was a banker and so he was able to help them get a mortgage. This remained the family home for a number of years and it was here on the 24th August 1958 that Jeannette Morton, the youngest of the three daughters, was born.

Marion, Jeannette, Inez (Agnes)

Allister and Jean's involvement in the work did not simply mean preaching and teaching, although they devoted much of their time to preaching the Gospel in those early days. Jean often spoke at ladies meetings or was involved in personal evangelism and tract distribution with the ladies, while Allister often travelled into remote villages to preach the gospel to many who had never heard the great message of salvation. Many of these remote villages could only be reached either by dug-out canoe or by mule. When Allister went on trips with the evangelists, often they had to hack their way through the bush with machetes as there were no roads, only narrow trails. Generally speaking, the villagers showed great hospitality though they had little they could offer, and time and again they expressed deep appreciation to their visitors for coming to bring them the Word of God. Their houses were built of dried mud blocks with earth floors, no running water of course and only an oil lamp for light. In the tropics night time comes quickly and where the village was surrounded by forest the darkness was almost palpable. In many cases chickens or pigs were included in the household which meant that there would be lice and ticks galore to keep the visitors company. On one such visit to a mountain village called Santa Maria, the owner of the house was a Christian and at night-time vacated his bed for Allister's "comfort" while he and his wife slept on a grass mat on the floor. (The "bed" by the way was made of dried animal skin nailed to a wooden frame). A few days before Allister had arrived, a crop of corn had just been harvested and that occupied a part of the house as well. During the night Allister was conscious of noises coming from the pile of corn. He soon realized what the noises were when rats ran across his body to get to and from the corn as he lay trying to sleep. These folks lived in abject poverty nevertheless they were willing to sacrifice what they had in order to give what little they did have to the "visitor", even denying themselves their meagre rations in order to do so.

Dugout Canoes

A typical jungle home

Visiting these remote villages not only entailed some dangerous travel through inhospitable jungle or bush, rivers and mountains, but where there were roads, these were either muddy or dusty, depending on the season and were peppered with huge pot holes. The roads were often narrow, as they were carved out of the mountainside with a steep precipice to the other side. Many an accident occurred when two overloaded trucks tried to pass on the hairpin bends that were an integral part of the journey. The trucks would usually have passengers crammed in every space inside, hanging on ledges on the outside and even sitting on the roof holding on to the luggage. Not only so, but many of the passengers had chickens and even pigs with them. The drivers did not have or hold to any rules of the road other than, "I got here first, so you reverse and let me pass"!

Many of the men would also carry guns and they were not averse to shooting them in the air to show off how macho they were or to celebrate something. On occasion they also used to shoot each other in a fight. Many also carried large sword-like knives called machetes. These were mainly used to chop down undergrowth or to kill snakes; however, there were also times when they too were used in anger or in a drunken fight.

These trips to remote villages were to prove very worthwhile because over time many people were brought to know the Lord and a number of small assemblies began to be established in these remote areas. During a visit by Allister and Jean to Jim and Olive Scollon, in La Ceiba on the North Coast of the country, the suggestion was made that they should go and encourage the Christians living in a town called Masica where a small assembly had been established. An evangelist and his wife, Pedro and Mariana Decorado, lived and worked in Masica, so Jim thought it would be opportune for Allister and Jean, who laboured in the interior of the country, to meet up with the Decorados. Although the town was not too far from the Scollon residence, nevertheless the journey would be through the dense bush because at that time there was no road from La Ceiba to Masica. It also meant fording various creeks as well as a river. However, the weather was fine with the water level in the creeks and river quite low presenting no immediate problem for Jim Scollon's brand new four wheel drive Jeep. Here is Allister's account of the visit;

"Olive Scollon and Alfreda Hockings had made sandwiches and coffee plus fruit juice for the children. This, of course, delighted the children to think that they were going to have a picnic lunch. Not long into the journey the children and the rest of us were happily singing choruses and handing out gospel literature to pedestrians on the road.

We finally arrived in Masica rejoicing that we encountered no problem crossing the creeks and the river. No prior notice of our visit had been given to Don Pedro or the assembly (in those early days of the work communications were difficult as there were no phones to let anyone know we were coming) The missionary/evangelist just "dropped in" and stayed for whatever length of time the people had available. On our arrival and after enjoying the picnic lunch, don Pedro went around the town telling everyone that there would be a meeting and that everyone was invited to hear a gospel message. The hall filled up quickly and when everyone was settled down, Jim Scollon gave the first message. Then I followed with my message, but before I had properly started, brother Scollon made frantic signs for me to stop as a freak rainstorm was sweeping down the mountain and he wanted to cross the river before it got too deep. One of the brethren closed with a word of prayer commending us to the Lord, and in a short time we packed our things into the car and headed off home. By this time it was intensely dark and when we got to the river, Jim slipped the car into four-wheel drive. Although the river was beginning to rage, Jim was confident that he could get across. On entering the water, the force of the water turned the car facing up-river and then the car became wedged on a boulder with the river rising quickly. Tree trunks, animals and rocks were all rushing down in the force of the flash flood. The water rose higher and higher and it became impossible to open any of the doors due to the pressure of the water. We did manage to open one window and I (Allister) was able to get out and began to help the others get out beginning with our youngest daughter (Jeannette one year old) and left her on the road. Then Marion (seven year old) was next and was left with Jeannette while I returned to get Agnes (ten year old) out. Jean was next and so as she saw to the girls, I helped Alfreda to get out. Jim by this time had managed to get out of the car. Finally, Olive got freed and joined the others on the road, with the rain coming down in torrents and no shelter of any kind to protect us. A woman and man appeared and kindly invited us to shelter in their humble shack till the rain subsided.

As we had travelled roughly between three and five kilometers from Masica, I volunteered to return there and seek help to get the car out of the river before it was carried downstream by the force of the water. Fortunately, a construction road crew had a camp on the outskirts of Masica with heavy-duty trucks and when I told the workers of our problem, the foreman in charge immediately gave the order for one of the drivers to take chains and assist us. On returning to the river I was able to get a chain on the tow-bar of our vehicle and eventually we got the Jeep out of the river. Unfortunately, the driver was unable to tow us back to the construction camp as the road was too slippery due to the mud, so both vehicles were abandoned till the morning as it was now too dark to do anything further. Our evangelist, don Pedro, opted to stay the night to make sure that no one would damage either vehicle. Jim and I thought it best for all of us to head back on foot to Masica as we were already soaking wet and our roadside friends' shack was too small to accommodate us all. With Jeannette on my shoulder and Marion and Agnes being cared for by Alfreda and Olive, we set off for Masica. It took us almost four hours slipping and sliding all the way until we finally arrived at Mariana's house. This dear sister had lit a big fire in anticipation of our return to Masica and had hot milk prepared for the children while their clothes were drying at the fire. Mariana told us that once we had left, the dear saints had a special prayer-meeting that the Lord would protect us from all harm knowing that flash-floods can be so dangerous. To God be the glory!

The following day, Jean, Olive and Alfreda with the three children retuned home by bus while Jim and I were towed back to La Ceiba by a passing fellow-missionary. Truly, our Lord Jesus was faithful to His promise: Fear not, for lo I am with you alway and will neither leave you nor forsake you! What a wonderful Saviour.

CHAPTER SEVEN

Opening Doors to Evangelism

Another area of service enabling young people to be reached with the gospel was camp work. In the early 1960s Mrs Ruddock (Aunt Nettie), had begun working with girls at camps. Here the girls enjoyed fun, games, good food, fellowship and activities, as well as hearing about God's love for them. Many of these young girls became Christians as a result of the camps and many have gone on to serve God since. Along with other missionaries, Allister and Jean continued to develop the camp work to include camps for boys as well as girls and three major campsites were developed; one in Tela, one in Trujillo and one in Valle de Angeles. Camps ran over the course of 5-6 weeks and as many as 1500 children and young people attended these and therefore heard God's word.

Girls camp in Tela

One of Allister's famous sayings has always been; "our aim is to be done out of a job" and to that end there were also camps held for the brethren so that they had a sound knowledge of God's word and would in time be able to take over the work themselves. These camps looked at the scriptures in depth and gave many young men the opportunity to preach and teach. Men would come from far and near often sacrificing to attend but at the end were equipped to return to their own small assemblies to teach and preach. This method has been very successful and later Allister was invited to go to Peru to show how it could work there too.

The camp at Valle, mens' Bible Study

At work in the camp kitchen

As well as teaching the girls, Jean was often to be found hard at work in the kitchen preparing food for the many hungry mouths. Some of the kitchens were fairly well equipped but others were very primitive and made the job of feeding so many people very difficult. For many of these children who came from poor homes, it was an experience that they were never to forget.

On one occasion Allister had to transport a number of girls from the capital city in the interior of the country to the coastal area where a camp was being held. These girls had never seen a railway engine in their life. There was one point on the road where the railway line crossed the road on which they were travelling. As the car came to the junction, a train was about to cross their path but because of the dense forestation the engine was hidden from view until it crossed in front of them. The poor girls got the fright of their life thinking they had seen a horrible monster that blew volumes of smoke from its head, and making ear-shattering noises as it thundered past them. Then, on reaching the coast, another surprise awaited them as they had never seen the ocean before. Doubtless, they must have thought they had come to the edge of the world. These campsites continue to be improved and upgraded and even today are touching the lives of young people in Honduras in a very special way.

Clay oven in a kitchen

Kitchen at Camp

As medical facilities were both scarce and expensive, people who lived in remote villages or who had no money had no access to medical treatment. From time to time they were blessed by visits from Doctors and Dentists who came mainly from the USA and Canada, to give of their time and expertise free of charge. When these medical and dental safaris took place, Jean and Allister were always ready and willing to go along with them to help in practical ways, but mainly to act as interpreters. Jean enjoyed this aspect of her work as she had always had a great interest in medical issues and she was not only a great help to the doctors and dentists, but she gained many medical skills and knowledge too. Allister would also act as the go-between for the medical team and the local authorities and at the same time taking the opportunity to speak to the people about God's love for them. The teams normally stayed for two weeks and during their stay, usually in harsh living conditions, hundreds of patients were helped who would never otherwise have been seen by a doctor or dentist.

Doctors working with patients

A dentist hard at work

Being a Missionary means being able to turn your hand to just about anything whether or not you are trained for it or you have the stomach for it! In Allister and Jean's case this often included dressing corpses. In tropical countries when a person dies, decomposition of the body takes place very quickly and burial usually takes place within 24 hours. In cities and larger towns there are funeral parlours that attend to embalming the body and the placing of the body in the coffin. This is a costly process beyond the pocket of the poor. So, poorer families generally have to attend to this ritual themselves; however, not all are willing to touch or dress a corpse. Enter the missionary! It may be 2 am in the morning, but within a short period of time, the word goes around and people begin to arrive at the house for the "wake". If the family was not Christian, everyone started to wail and cry, but if they were Christian then those present started to sing, read the Scriptures and comfort the bereaved. In the meantime, someone went out to buy a coffin, if not already purchased, and the missionary usually had to dress the corpse (if no one else is willing to do so), with the best suit or dress as the occasion demanded. The men went ahead to the burial ground to dig the grave and a member of the immediate family would go to the municipal building to register the death and obtain permission to bury the dead. Allister would then be asked to take the funeral service. Even today in the rural areas this would still be the way things work.

There were also many funny incidents like the story Allister tells below:

"We were living at the time in the second city of the country, San Pedro Sula, having taken over from our colleagues Jim and Vera Pugmire. Jim did not enjoy good health, and on this occasion he and Vera were planning to return to England on an extended furlough. He asked me if I could take over his radio work while he was away so that there would be a continuity of radio messages in his absence. Jean and I made the necessary arrangements to be in their home and to help in the assembly till they would return to Honduras. Unfortunately, the city of San Pedro is not the coolest of places to live in as the temperature constantly hovers around the 35°C (96°F) to 42°C (110°F). Scarcity of water is a major problem at all times with rivers and water holes dried up and is especially irksome when someone is going to be baptized.

Two or three months into our stay in San Pedro several believers had asked for baptism and so the elders decided on a date for the occasion. All that week it had been extremely hot, and I was rather anxious about the water situation, so I went to the hall to prepare for the baptisms and to make sure that there would be sufficient water in the baptistry. On arriving at the hall I saw that everything was ready but when I looked into the tank, my worst fears were confirmed - there was NO WATER! I phoned the elder who was responsible to see that the tank was full and suggested we call off the baptisms until such times that there would be sufficient water. However, the dear brother told me that the baptisms would take place as scheduled. The time was barely one hour away for the service to commence and the hall was all but filled with believers who wanted to witness the baptisms but there was NO WATER! The responsible brother then appeared with a smile on his face and assured me that we were going to go ahead with the baptisms as planned. "Without water in the tank?" I asked. "Oh no", he replied, "you will see". At that precise moment I heard the siren of a fire-engine coming down the street, stopping at the hall and then in came two firemen with a hose and filled the empty tank. The dear brother was well known to the fire department and had asked permission of the chief beforehand to use the fire-engine just for that purpose. Strange things can happen in Honduras! O ye of little faith!"

CHAPTER EIGHT

A New Chapter Begins

Jean and the three girls returned to Scotland in 1963 and lived for approximately 1 year in Greenock with Jean's mother. During that period of time Allister remained in Honduras but then re-joined the family in Scotland. The girls went to school initially in Greenock, then later, as the family had now moved to Gourock where they were able to purchase a small terraced house, they attended the High School there. While living in Gourock both Allister and Jean were in happy fellowship with the saints in Bethany Hall who were then constructing their new Hall. In 1966 Allister, Jean and Jeannette returned to Honduras and Inez and Marion remained in Scotland with Jean's mother who was a widow. Inez began her nurse's training and Marion attended Secondary School firstly in Largs High School and then in Ardrossan Academy for her fifth and sixth years of school.

On their return to Honduras Allister and Jean went to live in Tegucigalpa where they saw three more assemblies formed in the area as a result of the numerical growth of the main assembly at barrio La Guadalupe. The first new assembly was formed in Colonia 21, a new government housing project to accommodate the ever expanding population in the city. A number of believers in fellowship in the Guadalupe assembly were able to purchase houses and they started to hold gospel meetings in the colony. A number of the residents were converted to the Lord. A plot of ground was purchased in the colony where another gospel hall was built and soon was functioning with its own group of elders.

Stan and Esma Hanna from the USA who arrived in Honduras in 1958 were responsible for the second new assembly in La Travesia in a different area of the city. As some of the believers in fellowship in the Guadalupe assembly were from that part of the city they were encouraged to evangelise their neighbours. Soon the gospel message took root and some neighbours accepted the Lord Jesus as their Saviour and Lord. Stan and Esma played a great role, not only ministering to the saints, but also in building the gospel hall which today houses the assembly for their various meetings.

Another colony was built by the city and was called Colonia Rodriguez. Again gospel meetings were held in the open air which proved fruitful with some conversions among the neighbours who later were baptized and brought into fellowship. A plot of ground was purchased and soon the third new gospel hall was built.

In December 1971 Allister suffered a serious heart attack and was hospitalized for 18 days. As Inez had just completed her nursing training she flew out to Honduras to be at the side of her dad. Once stabilized, the family returned to Scotland and Inez was able to continue her nursing career as a midwife. The Doctors were not sure about a return to Honduras and so the family settled in Largs, in Ayrshire. Allister found work with the Red Cross, where there was a work-shop for handicapped people. His job was to prepare these handicapped people by showing them how to use their skills in a work-place environment. The firm, IBM, stationed in Greenock was extremely helpful in this respect because they passed on some assembly work that the handicapped workers were shown how to do. When they reached the point of proficiency, the assembled units were then returned to IBM. Other business men also made use of these workers so there was always work on hand which meant that they were now earning a wage for themselves giving them a measure of dignity and independence. Actually, some obtained such a degree of proficiency that employers were willing to employ them in the work-force.

CHAPTER NINE

The Return

During this time-period, in 1974 a devastating hurricane hit Honduras where Allister and Jean had been labouring for the Lord. Allister felt compelled to return to Honduras to help in relief work.

However, he was advised to have a thorough medical check-up prior to leaving and was told by the doctor that he would give him permission to go for three months. The Red Cross willingly granted him leave of absence and so Allister, accompanied by his friend and fellow-missionary, Sam Hanlon, returned to Honduras for the stipulated three months. It proved to be a rigorous undertaking, emotionally as well as physically. On returning to Scotland and having been checked on arrival by the cardiologist, Allister and Jean were exercised, after much serious prayer and consultation with their commending assemblies (Ardrossan & Saltcoats) to go back again to Honduras. In 1975 having been deemed fit to return to Honduras, Allister and Jean made the necessary plans to leave their youngest daughter, Jeannette, in Scotland. As Marion and Kenneth were married and living in Cumbernauld, Jeannette and her cousin Janice also came to live in Cumbernauld not too far from where Marion and Kenneth lived. She began her training to become a physiotherapist at this time.

Arriving back in Honduras Allister and Jean went to stay in San Pedro Sula to take over the radio ministry from Jim and Vera Pugmire so that they could take a well-deserved furlough in England. The radio ministry was commenced by

Jim and Vera about 1962 using a local commercial station which then was very restricted in its outreach. It served the local assemblies within a certain radius from the city of San Pedro Sula but no further. After some time, a new and powerful evangelical radio station was established in the capital city of Tegucigalpa which covered most of Central America and one could buy time at a reasonable rate. Sound bible teaching was given using this new station, much to the joy of believers who were living in mountainous and isolated areas of the country and were being denied such teaching on a regular basis. The radio work today is being carried on by brother David Dominguez.

Jim preparing his messages

Vera working the machines

After the Pugmires returned to Honduras to continue the radio work in San Pedro Sula, Allister and Jean moved back to Tegucigalpa to work closely with Stan and Esma Hanna (USA). The Hannas had been labouring for the Lord in Nicaragua for roughly two years when a civil war erupted in that country and they had to leave and return to Honduras. They concentrated on building up the new assembly that had been formed in la Travesia, while Allister and Jean gave help to the new assembly in la Colonia 21 as well as to the main assembly meeting in barrio la Guadalupe.

At this time, Manuel Nasralla donated about ten acres of ground for a campsite in the village of Valle de Angeles about 22 kilometres distant from the capital city of Tegucigalpa. As many of the brethren in fellowship were in the building industry, they, along with the missionaries, began to build brick cabins where the future camp attendees would be housed. Allister's knowledge of plumbing proved to be an asset when it came to installing the toilets and the showers as well as the drainage. For many future campers, especially those who lived in small and isolated villages up in the mountains, these toilets would be something of a mystery at first sight until they were accustomed to using them.

Today, the camp has been used extensively by all the different age-groups from the different assemblies throughout the country, and over the years a good number of those who attended came to a saving knowledge of the Lord Jesus. Many of these young people, became the counsellors and preachers at future camps, as they grew in grace and in the knowledge of the Truth.

In the year 1980, John and Nettie Ruddock, who were then labouring for the Lord in the coastal town of Tela, retired from the field. During their stay in Tela, John and Nettie were exercised to build a home for some of the aged saints who had no one to care for them. Not only had these elderly saints a comfortable place to stay where they were given three good meals each day, the home was also adjacent to the Gospel Hall so they did not have far to walk for the meetings. Two young sisters in fellowship were employed to cook the food and clean out the rooms each day while Nettie saw to any necessary health needs. In 1980 when the Ruddocks retired, Allister and Jean felt exercised to move to Tela to oversee the administration of the Home. This move also gave Allister an opportunity to visit extensively all along the North Coast where many assemblies had been formed by the testimony of the native evangelists and faithful believers.

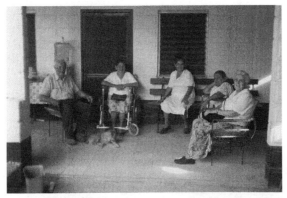

Allister and Jean visiting the seniors at the Home in Tela, 2006

Allister with the senior gentleman at the Home in Tela, 2006

For the next six years they remained at the Old Folks Home in Tela, till in 1986 Mr Jim Scollon passed away.

Jim and his wife Olive had established a wonderful work producing resources to enable the Christians to grow in their faith and had a printing press in the town of La Ceiba further along the coast. It was to continue this work and to help the Assembly in La Ceiba that Allister and Jean felt called.

Allister became the Assistant Editor of the magazine 'Verdades Biblicas' or 'Bible Truths'. Even in his retirement Allister continued to write over a number of years. Many lives were touched and faith strengthened through the reading of this magazine.

Jim and Olive Scollon at the printing press

Jim and Olive with Mr and Mrs Hockings

CHAPTER TEN

The Next Stage of The Journey

As Allister continued to have recurring health problems, in March 1992 they finally took the advice that it was time to retire from the work and the heat. So after 42 years of faithful service, Allister and Jean moved to Vancouver to be with their youngest daughter Jeannette and her husband and family, where they live to this day.

As soon as they arrived in Vancouver, Allister and Jean found a new spiritual home in Surrey Gospel Chapel. This opened a new chapter in their service as they became more and more involved in the life and work of the assembly. Allister became an elder while Jean was called upon to give help in the Sunday school, as well as ministering to the sisters. Other avenues for ministry began to open up as time went by. Both Allister and Jean were called upon to minister in the many surrounding assemblies in the Vancouver area as well as to travel further afield to other Provinces in Canada to preach the Word.

Two new venues within Vancouver itself were to become another outreach for Allister and Jean, where their knowledge of the Spanish language proved to be an asset. These were; the Union Gospel Mission (UGM) and the Lighthouse Harbour Ministries (LHM). A brother in the Lord, Doug Fraser, invited Allister to accompany him to the Surrey Fraser Docks to visit the incoming ships where many of the seamen were from Spanish speaking countries. From then on, both Allister and Jean went regularly to the docks to intermingle with the off-duty seamen and to present the gospel to them.

However, although formally retired from Honduras their hearts remained there and in June 1993 they returned for an intensive three months. During these three months Allister worked with Stan Hanna to deliver in depth Bible studies in Acts with a number of the newer churches. These studies took place during the day and then they had outreach meetings in the evenings. At the end of the course there was an exam for the students. In the longest established assembly in Guadalupe (Tegucigalpa), they also had studies on Discipleship and The Holy Spirit.

In 1995 Allister returned alone for four months travelling around the various Assemblies preaching and teaching. But 1998 saw them both return to Honduras for a further three months where this time both Allister and Jean were involved in taking meetings in Tela, Trujillo and Tegucigalpa. In October of that visit they were involved at a big weekend conference where Jean spoke to the ladies. She also spoke at a Ladies Conference in Valle de Angeles and they were both involved in meetings for young people.

It was during this visit that hurricane Mitch hit causing devastating damage with a high loss of life due to flooding and mudslides. Allister and Jean managed to get out on the last commercial flight as the runway was damaged and only flights bringing aid were being allowed to use it. On their return they quickly set about raising awareness in the Assemblies both on the East and West sides of Canada. The Assemblies responded very generously and soon two 40ft containers were filled with useful goods to go to help those worst affected by the devastation of Hurricane Mitch. Allister went back to Honduras and remained for a further 2 months helping with the reconstruction of homes and assembly buildings, as well as encouraging the believers.

In the year 2000, they returned once again to Honduras for a few weeks of conferences and to visit old friends and colleagues. This time they took with them Marion's younger daughter, Cheryl, who was going to spend her gap year before going to university to study medicine. This proved to be a very beneficial year for Cheryl as she worked with an American lady Doctor who had a clinic in one of the very poor areas of the town of La Ceiba. Here Cheryl saw and was able to practise many simple procedures that she would otherwise have had to wait till well into her course to do. She was very saddened by the poverty that she saw and once commented that the saddest thing was that for many they had nothing, not even hope. In that year she also managed to grasp the basics of Spanish and after some time in La Ceiba she moved to Tegucigalpa where she helped out in a Christian school in the mountains. It allowed her the opportunity to get to know the country where her mother had been born and had spent the majority of her childhood. It also helped her to grow in confidence, gain experience and grow in her faith. It was during this year that she was baptized.

In 2001, Allister was invited by missionaries, Eric and Donna McKinley, to visit the work in Peru and to give them some advice and guidance about how he, with others, had set up the teaching and Bible studies for Elders and National Workers. He took with him two of the Elders from Honduras who, along with Allister had been involved in the setting up of that aspect of the work in Honduras. He remained there for a month and they had a profitable time together.

Once again in 2002 Allister returned to his adopted homeland for a further short visit. This time Jean remained in Canada, but later in 2006 both Allister and Jean had another visit to Honduras. A report of this visit was featured in Echoes of Service magazine some time later and it is included in the following chapter.

CHAPTER ELEVEN

Honduras Revisited

Honduras Revisited

"After having laboured for forty years in Honduras, the Lord opened the door for Jean and me to re-visit the country for a short time. It was not in the sense of a vacation but rather a "home going". We left Canada on 4th October and returned on the 28th October 2006. It had been our intention to stay for a longer period of time, but my health put a limit on just how long we could stay. The words of Paul to Barnabas echoed our real sentiments when he said, "Let us now go back and visit our brethren in every city where we have preached the Word of the Lord and see how they are doing". So I thought I should take this opportunity to give a brief summary as to "how they (the believers in Honduras) are doing".

A TOUCH OF NOSTALGIA

On our arrival in the country, the first meeting that evening was held in Suyapa, a suburb of the capital city of Tegucigalpa where the Dominguez (US) labour for the Lord. During our stay in Tegucigalpa we were graciously hosted by the Woolers. (US) The annual general conference for believers had been arranged from the 8th to the 10th of October with the venue in Tegucigalpa where Jean and I had laboured from 1951 till 1980. Over 700+ believers from the various assemblies within the country attended the conference which, for us, was very emotional. We saw some older believers that we had known forty or fifty years ago when they trusted in the Lord as their Saviour, and today are still standing firm in their testimony and witnessing to their neighbors.

We observed quite a few changes that rejoiced our hearts. The work of the Lord is now in the indigenous mode with the believers themselves doing the evangelism, and though there are still four missionary couples and two single sisters on the field, (all from USA) by and large, each one of the 300+ assemblies is completely autonomous with its own oversight and outreach program. The Lord continues to bless richly in the gospel outreaches with souls being baptized and brought into fellowship. The foreign missionaries still in the country occupy a supportive role by visiting the assemblies but do not interfere with the schedules as set out by the oversight of the individual assemblies. Often they are called upon by an assembly, or group of assemblies, as the case might be, to give ministry to the saints on given subjects such as marriage, or specific doctrines relating to Church Truth, or prophesy, or to give ministry at conferences, etc.

Several local assemblies are now sending missionaries to the neighbouring countries of Nicaragua, Guatemala, and Costa Rica and supporting them financially. This had ever been our objective in the first place on going to Honduras with the gospel, that one day the work would ultimately pass into the hands of the brethren, themselves. Now that objective has come round in a complete circle. Truly, "This is the Lord's doing and is marvelous in our eyes." Yes, "Not unto us O Lord, but unto Thy Name give glory." In spite of the increasing wickedness within the country, such as drug cartels, immorality, and violence, and in the spiritual realm, false sects seeking to undermine the faith of the saints, nevertheless, each local assembly is standing fast in the Truth letting its light shine in the darkness by calling on men to repent and believe the gospel. God is, indeed, using the testimony of these assemblies in all of Latin America, and many precious souls have recently come to know Him Whom to know is life eternal as a result of their witness.

In the year 1960, the then president of the country, Dr. Villeda Morales, declared that over 70% of the people were illiterate. His wife, doña Alejandrina who was a school teacher, vowed that the Government would make it compulsory for all children to have at least a basic education up to 6th grade level, even in the most remote villages. Today, schools are full, and illiteracy has all but disappeared. Two missionary couples, the Hannas and the Dominguez, were led to build a school in the respective towns where each was located, one in Trujillo on the North Coast of the country, and the other in Suyapa in the interior. Although they follow the Government curriculum they have the liberty to teach the Word of God to the students. The school in Trujillo has an attendance of 100+ students going from 1st grade to 9th grade who are, by and large, boarders at the school. Mrs Hanna is still an active participant at the school. The majority of the teachers profess to be believers in the Lord Jesus. In Suyapa, over 250 students are enrolled and the Dominguez are hoping to extend their enrolment up to 12th grade. Many of the students in both schools are now rejoicing in the knowledge that their sins have been forgiven. Also in Valle de Angeles as well as in La Ceiba, the local assembly in each town runs a Kindergarten from pre-school to 2nd grade with the purpose of adding one grade each year. All the assembly-run schools, have received high praise from Government Inspectors, with the result that parents are desirous of enrolling their children in the assembly-run schools.

RADIO WORK

The use of radio in the field of evangelism was commenced by the Pugmires many years ago, using a commercial station to air the various programmes. Unfortunately, the commercial station failed to air the message at the contracted time especially when there was a soccer game in progress, or some other function, and aired it when they considered it convenient to do so. This was rather disconcerting to the believers who tuned in at the time the program was due to be aired, only to find that it had been moved to an unknown time. Finally, a brother set up his own local radio station and although limited in its outreach, it was considered superior to the commercial one because it kept to the advertised time. This dear brother uses it exclusively for the preaching of the gospel as well as for ministry to the believers on the coastal region of the country. Although I was roughly 380 kilometers away, this brother phoned me and asked me to give a message of greeting to his listeners. "You are on the air" he told me, "the lines are open so go ahead. I am holding the telephone to the microphone". On a second occasion he told me that many of the believers who had been listening had phoned in asking that I give a word of ministry there and then. Yes, one has to be "always ready to give an answer to every man that asks you a reason of the hope that is in you". Among the believers there is great hunger for the Word of the Lord and they are ready to drop whatever they happen to be doing in order to have a meeting.

EMMAUS COURSES

The Emmaus Bible courses are used extensively and normally when the believers do tract distribution there is an invitation included for the recipient to get the first course free. These courses have been used by the Spirit of God to speak to prisoners in prisons as well as those in the neighbourhood. God is working powerfully in Honduras as well as in the other countries of Central America. Let us remember these dear saints of God in supportive prayer!"

Prior to writing that previous article for Echoes of Service, the email below was sent to the Bath office of Echoes of Service and as it has some additional detail, I have included it.

Dear Brethren,

Both Jean and I are grateful for the many prayers of the saints that rose to the throne of grace on our behalf during our recent visit to our former field of service in Honduras. Four things motivated the visit: firstly, we were invited to participate in the conference to celebrate the 50th Anniversary of the inauguration of the first Gospel Hall to be constructed in the capital of the Republic. Secondly, I had been invited to participate in a Bible study for Elders. Thirdly, Jean had been asked to address the Sisters' camp, and fourth, it was my desire to visit the neighbouring country of Nicaragua where the assemblies had recently commenced evangelizing.

Having arrived in Honduras toward the end of 1950, we commenced the study of the Spanish language in the town of Tela on the north coast of the country. Roughly nine months later, a dear brother in Tegucigalpa invited us to consider going to the capital to care for a fledgling assembly of twelve believers then meeting in his home. Believing this to be a "Macedonian call to come over and help us", we then moved to the capital in 1951 after an initial visit, found a two-story house suitable for both a dwelling place for our needs (upstairs) and for future meetings (downstairs). After returning from our first furlough, in 1956 we commenced the construction of the hall which was inaugurated in October 1956. Since then, with the Lord's blessing and with the help of fellow-missionaries who worked alongside us, there are now seven assemblies in different parts of the City. "This is the Lord's doing and it is wonderful in our eyes" - "Not unto us, O Lord, but unto Thy Name give glory".

Approximately 400 believers attended the conference and when the conference ended, six believers were baptized. (Three weeks later a further six were baptized in the assembly meeting in the barrio of Suyapa on the outskirts of Tegucigalpa.) Jean and I then drove to the north coast with our colleagues, the Hannas, to the City of Trujillo where the Bible study for Elders was to take place. About forty elders were present from different assemblies when two full-time evangelists, don Concepcion Padilla and don Jonatan Nunez along with myself, ministered to them relating to eldership and the autonomy of the local church. A very touching moment took place that moved me deeply. About half way through the studies, we learned that the funeral of dear Sam Hanlon was to take place that day and so the brethren spent half-an-hour praying for Edna and the family. Sam had played a very big part in the lives of most of these dear brethren, and he was held by them in high esteem. After the studies, I was able to visit various assemblies along the north coast and had a precious time ministering to them.

Thereafter we returned to Tegucigalpa where it was Jean's turn to minister to between 75 - 100 sisters at the Camp grounds in Valle de Angeles 20 kilometres to the east of the city. She was joined by a dear sister, Maria Darling, from Houston, U.S.A. whose husband had laboured for the Lord in Cuba but who is now with the Lord. While Jean was at the camp, I went to Nicaragua where that country had already been visited by Stan and Esma Hanna in the 1970s, but after labouring for two years, had to withdraw due to the civil war. A young Honduran believer was led to visit Nicaragua at weekends to preach the Word. He was followed a number of years later by a dear sister from New Zealand, Helen Goatley, who worked among the prostitutes in the city of Managua. After that, two missionary families, the Ferrers and the Reeves, went from Honduras to Nicaragua, and now there are seven assemblies raised to the glory of God.

Honduran assemblies have now commended seven couples to the work in Nicaragua whom they support financially and prayerfully. In recent times, two other families have gone into Nicaragua, one from Canada (the Bacherts) and one from the States (the Fletts whose brother and his wife labour for the Lord in El Salvador). Do New Testament principles work in the 21st century? Most assuredly they do! Yes, again we say, "Not unto us, O Lord, but unto Thy Name give glory" "We are unprofitable servants. We have done what was our duty to do".

According to David Dominguez, labouring in Tegucigalpa, at the time of writing this email there were 267 assemblies in Honduras. The native evangelists are taking the gospel to all areas of Honduras, and not only confining the preaching to Hondurans, but to the neighbouring countries as well, even traveling as far south as Panama where some contacts have been already made. God is doing a mighty work in Latin America. Brethren, keep on praying to the Lord of the harvest to use these dear brethren and sisters in the salvation of precious souls and for the planting of new assemblies.

Your servant for Christ's sake,

Allister and Jean

They managed to make two further trips, one in 2009 and what became their final visit in 2010.

In a recent conversation with a brother from Honduras, Allister was informed that in the town of Tela, where they had served for many years in the Old Folks Home and the Assembly, there are now six assemblies where previously there were two and that across the whole country there are now around 400 assemblies! These have almost totally been added due to the work of the National Evangelists and local Christians. Allister's comment to that was that he is very happy that the missionaries have been done out of a job as that was always their goal; to hand the work over to the local Christians. What an amazing God we have! He truly is in control.

Christians attending a conference

CHAPTER TWELVE

Testimonies

As it is not possible to include all the testimonies of the many men, women and even children who came to faith in the Lord Jesus Christ during their years in Honduras, below are a few examples of some of these believers' conversion stories.

Dr. Bermudez

In the city of La Ceiba on the North Coast of Honduras lived a Christian couple, Oscar and Nora Morazán, who were very zealous for the Lord. Nora worked as a secretary in the general hospital that was directed by Dr. Bermudez who was a brother of the wife of the President of Honduras. He had previously occupied the position as Ambassador of Honduras to London as well as holding other important posts during his tenure in the diplomatic service, but since his retirement from that service, Dr. Bermudez returned to his profession as medical doctor and was now in charge of the hospital.

On one occasion, Dr. Bermudez spoke to Nora and told her that she appeared to have something he did not have. At first, Nora was somewhat puzzled and asked him what he meant by his remark. The doctor then told her that he had observed her on several occasions noting that she portrayed a tranquility that shone in her life and made her quite different from others he knew. Nora replied that she was a believer in the Lord Jesus and perhaps that was the difference. The doctor was called away at that point thus ending their conversation.

Some time later, Nora and the doctor met in the corridor of the hospital, and again Dr Bermudez repeated that she had something that he did not have and what could it be? This time Nora asked the doctor if it would be convenient if she and her husband could have an opportunity to clarify some verses in the bible, and to this he gladly agreed and invited them to come to his home. A convenient date was fixed for a meeting, and I was asked to accompany them. The doctor and his wife were very open to study the Word of God in spite of the fact that they were of the Roman Catholic persuasion. Having established our friendship with the Bermudez family, Jean and I became regular visitors to their home and they to ours, and our conversation always centred round the Scriptures of Truth. Finally, one night while Mrs. Bermudez and Jean were in a different room, I was able to lead the doctor, with the tears running down his cheeks, to faith in Christ.

A week or so passed when Dr. Bermudez had another encounter with Nora at the hospital and he said to her, "Nora, I have something to tell you" and she replied, "What do you want to tell me?" "I now have what you have". Nora, of course, feigned surprise when he said that he had trusted in the Lord as his Saviour, because we had already told her before-hand. "Not unto us, O Lord, but unto Thy Name give glory"

Tiburcio Rodriguez
I first met Tiburcio Rodriguez in the city of El Progreso on the North Coast of Honduras. He was well known in the city and in the surrounding villages as he had a most remarkable conversion and deliverance from his sinful past.

Before he met his Saviour, Tiburcio was affiliated to a gang where he spent his hard-earned cash drinking with his companions who were constantly engaged in fighting other rival gangs. On one particular occasion, three men of a rival gang found Tiburcio alone, and a fight ensued and using their sharp machetes they attacked him. Unfortunately, he was out-numbered and was left with his right arm completely cut off from his body and a deep machete wound across his face. When taken to the hospital, the doctor in attendance thought he had no hope of saving Tiburcio's life so he said he would stitch up his wounds as he would look better that way in his coffin. However, against all odds, he did survive and he vowed he would seek out and kill all three of his enemies once he was healed. On leaving the hospital, Tiburcio began using his left hand to do what he normally did with his right hand, especially when using his machete.

Having gained confidence in the use of his left hand he sought out his three enemies and did exactly what he had promised he would do. However, the Lord had His eye on Tiburcio and one day he heard the clear gospel message, which brought him to his knees in repentance and faith in Christ Jesus as his Lord and Saviour. With gang warfare behind him Tiburcio is now fighting the good fight of faith.

Don Enrique Carvajal

On returning to Honduras from our first furlough in 1956, a plot of land was purchased with the intention of building the first Gospel Hall in the capital city of Tegucigalpa. Previously we had utilized the large room in the building we rented, which at that moment in time, was large enough for the young church. However, the gospel outreach in the area saw more and more interest among the neighbours, with the result that there was insufficient room to seat all who were now attending the meetings.

Having purchased the plot of land, it was decided to commence the construction of the building. Local tradesmen, some of whom had started coming to the meetings, were used in the construction. Passersby would stop and ask what the building was going to be used for. One particular neighbour was a man called, Enrique Carvajal. He was surprised when one of the believers explained that it was to be used for the preaching of the gospel. The believer then invited don Enrique to attend the meetings once the building was completed, and this he promised to do. Faithful to his word, don Enrique was present at the inauguration of the hall and from that day on he seldom missed a meeting.

We were later to find out that don Enrique was a Colonel in the army and was one of the President of the country's right hand men. He was a nominal Roman Catholic but began showing a great interest every time he heard the message of God's love and mercy. Finally don Enrique accepted the Lord as his personal Saviour and was among the first to use the baptistry in the new hall. Being in the army, don Enrique had some old enemies and always carried his gun ready in his pocket. However, he was convicted by the Lord one day, that since he had trusted in the Lord for the well-being of his soul, why was he not willing to trust the Lord for physical protection? After giving it much consideration, don Enrique sold his pistols and settled down as a cattle-rancher and became a much-esteemed elder in his local assembly.

Omar Ortiz

Though not from a Christian family, as a young man Omar heard the gospel message and responded to it. Stan Hanna noted his interest and soon took him under his wings, to help him grow in his faith and knowledge of the scriptures. Stan and Esma would often open their home to young men who showed potential and needed and wanted to be instructed in God's word. They would stay with the family for a week or two getting daily exposure to God's word. He proved to be a very good student and soon began to preach. As he matured, he became an excellent preacher and before long he was commended to become a full time evangelist. He and his wife, Lesley, continue to serve the Lord and their people around the country. Lesley often worked with Jean at the ladies' camps and continues to be very active in the ladies' work. Omar and Lesley now have a grown up family, but here is a photograph of him as a young man with Stan Hanna and Allister.

Omar Ortiz with Allister and Stan

Doña Florinda de Nasralla

Doña Florinda and her husband lived next to John and Nettie Ruddock in Trujillo in the 1930s. They were very staunch Roman Catholics with Florinda being a teacher in the local convent. John and Nettie had not long been in Honduras and wanted to befriend them, in spite of a level of resistance to them talking about their need of being saved. It was a period of serious illness within the Nasralla family that helped to bond the friendship between Nettie and Florinda as Nettie was the only one willing to help and support them through this difficult time. As the friendship developed, the resistance to hearing the good news of salvation lessened and in time Florinda became a Christian. Later she was very keen to be baptised, but her husband was very much against that. However, Florinda felt that she needed to follow the word of God and be baptised. Her husband, Salvador, threatened to kill her if she got baptised, but in spite of that threat she went ahead. On the day of her baptism everyone was nervous about what would happen, as they had all heard about don Salvador's threat. As Florinda was being raised out of the water, Salvador walked into the hall and walked straight towards her. Everyone held their breath wondering if he would shoot her, but to their surprise and relief, he embraced her and told her that she was a very brave woman. His journey to faith began that day and he too became a Christian in due course. They had a family of seven children who also became Christians. One daughter Esma married Stan Hanna and they were missionaries in Honduras doing a great work for the Lord. Another sister America (Mecca) married Enrique Carvajal and they were very involved in their local assembly with Enrique becoming an elder. Although he was the eldest in the family, Manuel remained a very staunch Catholic and he was the last to become a Christian. The story of his conversion merits telling separately. So, Florinda's conversion led to the salvation of not only her husband and family, but also of the many others who were led to the Lord by the words and actions of her family in later years.

Manuel Nasralla
As in the story of Doña Florinda, Manuel resisted all attempts to convert him. He was a high flying young banker with Banco Atlantida in Tegucigalpa and his boss realized his potential, so he sent him to Palestine to work in Barclay's Bank there to gain more experience. Banco Atlantida was affiliated to Barclay's Bank and so he was able to work there for a time. Before leaving for Palestine John Ruddock handed him a Bible and asked him to read it. Manuel took the Bible and agreed to do so. The year was around 1940 and the war was in progress. Manuel remained in Palestine till 1947. As promised he read the Bible he had been given, but still resisted becoming a Christian, till one day he was

invited to a conference by one of the bank tellers and there at the conference he gave his life to the Lord. He returned to Honduras and met and married Anna McNab whose father was a sea captain whose family originally came from Scotland. Meantime in 1944, Allister's Air Force training had taken him to Palestine where he was billeted a very short distance away from the very place that Manuel was living. At this point in time of course, neither Allister nor Manuel knew each other nor had heard of each other, as Allister and Jean had not yet married, nor gone to Honduras. By the time Allister and Jean arrived in Honduras in 1950, Manuel and Anna were holding a small meeting in their home in Tegucigalpa. The couples were introduced and as they talked they realised that God had truly brought them together in this far away land to bring glory to His name. They soon became very firm friends, working together in the small assembly. The friendship with Anna continues to the point of writing and did with Manuel till his home-call in 1998.

Anna and Manuel Nasralla a few years before his homecall

CHAPTER THIRTEEN

The Family Today

Agnes (Inez) trained to be a nurse and then a midwife, in Glasgow, Scotland and was a great support when Allister had his first heart attack in 1971. She went to Honduras to be with her parents and there she met Roy Stefan, who later became her husband. She lived in Honduras thereafter and has four children. Roy passed away in 2013 and Inez now lives in Vancouver where her two daughters, Allison and Allain also live. Her two sons, Allister who is a pharmacist and Allan who is a doctor and their wives and families, remain in Honduras, so Inez makes return visits whenever possible. She also now has six grandchildren.

The wedding of Agnes and Roy

Marion trained to be a teacher and later went on to be a Head Teacher in two Private schools in Scotland where she lives with her husband Kenneth. Kenneth was a High School Principal and he continues as a consultant in education. They have two daughters, one of whom, Cheryl, spent a year in Honduras prior to going on to become a Doctor. She is married to Cliff, a Canadian. Their older daughter Pamela is in the teaching profession like her parents. Pamela and her husband, Robert, have two daughters.

The wedding of Marion and Kenneth

Jeannette trained to be a physiotherapist and moved to Canada when an opportunity arose to work in Regina. She met her husband, Don, a pilot and they married and settled firstly in Ottawa and then in Vancouver. They have four children, Brad who is also a pilot like his father and who recently married and now has a daughter, Darla, also married with two children and the two younger daughters, Joanne and Karen, who are still studying.

The wedding of Jeannette and Don

Marion and Jeannette have both made return trips to Honduras. All of the families have also gone for visits so that they are aware of and know about where their mothers grew up. Darla, like Cheryl, spent time in Honduras. Marion also went to La Mosquitia with a team from the Christian charity Tearfund, to see the work being undertaken with the indigenous people who live in the rainforest of La Mosquitia.

Honduras will always remain in their hearts and minds, particularly as both Marion and Jeanette were born there and although Inez was born in Scotland prior to Allister and Jean going to Honduras, she was the one who married and lived there for the majority of her adult life. All three girls look on Spanish as their first language and though nowadays they do not have cause to use it very often, it does from time to time come in very handy.

On Remembrance Day 2013, Allister was invited to participate in the celebration fly-past that the Canadian Air Force were doing in British Columbia. He and his grandson Brad, who is also a pilot, were welcomed as co-pilots in the Harvards as they went flying past each of the Cenotaphs in the Vancouver area. You can imagine the pleasure that gave an old pilot! His face was beaming with joy and pride. What a great gift to have given a 90 year old! Thanks to the Canadian Air Force for their kindness in allowing him that great pleasure and privilege.

In the air

2013 Remembrance Day Fly-by

CHAPTER FOURTEEN

90th Birthday Celebration

The North Surrey Assembly where Allister and Jean have worshipped since their arrival in Vancouver, held a service of celebration for them to commemorate not only their 90th birthdays, but more importantly, their service to God and His great faithfulness towards them.

Their three daughters were there with them to celebrate, as were many friends and fellow members of the assembly. The family would like to thank the assembly, not only for that lovely tribute, but also for their ongoing care, love and support over many years and especially now as age takes its toll.

Celebrating 90 years of God's faithfulness

Jean and Allister together at their 90th birthday celebration

*Jean and Allister with their three daughters
at their 90th birthday celebration*

Photos of the growing family

Some Honduran Artifacts

CHAPTER FIFTEEN

Photo Gallery

Early assembly outside their church hall

Barrio outside Tegucigalpa

A baptism in the river

A family picnic with friends (Sheddens and Nasrallas)

Early Assembly

Nasrallas, Sheddens and Haemskirks

Jungle inhabitant

The local market

Another day's washing done

Family at a missionary reunion at Netherhall, Largs

Local road in Tegucigalpa

A boy at work

Honduras 2006. Many from the first assembly in Tegucigalpa

Homes on the outskirts of Tegucigalpa

Members of the assembly at La Masica

The hall at La Masica

Doña Mariana and Don Pedro from La Masica

Travel in La Mosquitia

Captain Shedden
after a flight to Guatemala City
to pick up Inez who had been in
Los Angeles recuperating

Allister preaching in Honduras

Allister and Jean's Golden Wedding celebration in Vancouver, Canada with many of their family

Home in a poorer Barrio

Campamento Mixto 1987

Youth Camp Sports Team

All MK girls together

Boys camp using plantation before the new camps were built

Sam and Edna Hanlon with members of the Assembly

David and Lourdes Domingez